Michael Smith was born in Dublin in 1942. In 1967 he set up New Writers' Press with Trevor Joyce, with whom he also edited the seminal journal *The Lace Curtain*. Thus began a career that led to him becoming one of the leading Irish translators and poets of the past half century.

He has translated, mostly in collaboration with his friend, the Spanish scholar Luis Ingelmo, a wide range of Spanish-language writers including Federico García Lorca, Pablo Neruda, Miguel Hernández, Gerardo Diego, Luis Cernuda, Gustavo Adolfo Bécquer, Claudio Rodríguez, and Rosalía de Castro, along with the two Spanish masters of the baroque, Francisco de Quevedo and Luis de Góngora.

With the Peruvian scholar Valentino Gianuzzi, he has translated the complete poems of César Vallejo (Shearsman Books — collected in a single-volume edition in 2012). In 2014 Shearsman also published his translation (with Luis Ingelmo) of the Renaissance poet, Fernando de Herrera; Parlor Press (USA) will also soon publish his translation of *Magnetic Brackets* by the contemporary Spanish poet, Jesús Losada.

His achievement in translation was acknowledged in 2001 when he was awarded the European Academy Medal for Poetry. He has also published several volumes of his own poetry, which in turn has been widely translated — his *Collected Poems* were published by Shearsman in 2009. Michael Smith is a member of Aosdána (The National Irish Academy of Artists).

Also by Michael Smith at Shearsman Books

Poetry
 The Purpose of the Gift. Selected Poems.
 Collected Poems

Translations
 Maldon & Other Translations
 Rosalía de Castro: *Selected Poems*

With Luis Ingelmo

Translations
 Gustavo Aldolfo Bécquer: *Collected Poems (Rimas)*
 Elsa Cross: *Selected Poems*
  (with Anamaría Crowe Serrano & John Oliver Simon)
 Fernando de Herrera: *Selected Poems*
 Claudio Rodríguez: *Collected Poems / Poesía completa*
 José António Villacañas: *Selected Poems*
 Verónica Volkow: *Arcana & other poems*
 Poems from Other Tongues
 Cantes flamencos (Flamenco Songs)

With Valentino Gianuzzi

Translations
 César Vallejo: *The Complete Poems*
 César Vallejo: *Selected Poems*
 César Vallejo: *The Black Heralds & Other Early Poems*
 César Vallejo: *Trilce*
 César Vallejo: *Collected Later Poems 1923–1938*

Michael Smith

Prayers for the Dead

and other poems

Shearsman Books

First published in the United Kingdom in 2014 by
Shearsman Books
50 Westons Hill Drive
Emersons Green
BRISTOL
BS16 7DF

Shearsman Books Ltd Registered Office
30–31 St. James Place, Mangotsfield, Bristol BS16 9JB
(this address not for correspondence)

www.shearsman.com

ISBN 978-1-84861-337-9

Copyright © Michael Smith, 2014.
The right of Michael Smith to be identified as the author
of this work has been asserted by him in accordance with the
Copyrights, Designs and Patents Act of 1988.
All rights reserved.

ACKNOWLEDGEMENTS
Some of these poems have previously appeared in the following:
The Irish Times, Plume, Poetry Ireland Review, and the anthology,
If ever you go: A Map of Dublin in Poetry and Song.
My thanks to the editors.

*To Tony Frazer,
friend, supporter and publisher,
in that order.*

Contents

I Scenes of Deterrence

Library & Cemetery	11
Inner City Canal	13
Without Farewell	14
Of Crows in Time of Civil War	15
White Marble	16
The River	18
In the Ruins	19
The Old Windows	20
Portent	21
Rural Retreat	22
The White Swan	24
Village in the Mountains Long Ago	25
The Centenarian Trees	27
The People's City	28
Village Abattoir	29
The Haven I	31
The Haven II	33

II People, Present & Gone

Stoker Joe	37
Old Will Deceased	38
We Are Alive	39
Mystery Man	40
Barflies	41
Men under the Railway Bridge	42
Suicide	43
The Perfect Lady	44
An Unknown Life	45
Schoolboy Mitcher	46
Tu Fu in Templeogue	48
For My Eldest Sister Dead by Fire	50
I Am Happy, Happy	51

III The Poet

The Poet as Wild Man	55
The Gifted Poet	56
Death of a Poet	57
Fionn: The Poet As Truant	58
Common Birds	60
Sumer Is Icumen In	61
The Poet As Pub Singer	62
Trinity of Faces	63
Poet as Outsider	64
Death of an Old Poet	65

IV Reflections of a Sun to Come

The Envoy's Soliloquy	69
Of Youth And Age	71
Write Something Happy	73
Let's Soldier On	74
'La Vida Es Sueño'	75
The Greater Grace	76
Last Words of the Old Atheist	77
Major or Minor	78
Street Rhymes	79
A Single Word	81
Grey Rain	82
Lady Morphia	83
Castilian Rhymes	84
Winter Muse	85
Love Is the Unspoken	86

Author's Note

Let me try to define prayer as I am using it here. It is a voice in the head, ours and not ours. It speaks in words we scarcely understand. Unstoppable, unless distracted by our quotidian pursuits. Beckett said it thus: "All poetry, as discriminated from the various paradigms of prosody is prayer." Enigmatic, but what else would one expect from Beckett? Essentially, I perceive prayer as a form of homage or "recognition"—the other word used by Beckett.

I

Scenes of Deterrence

Library & Cemetery

i.m. Samuel Beckett

The library is now a cemetery of epitaphs:
books shelved, inert, awaiting the occasional visit.

Names trip on the tongue, major or minor,
in or out of fashions never foreseen.

Mostly a deafening silence is this abode
in withering summer sunlight or autumn dankness.

Voices in the mind not tongue when pages open,
little tricks of style habitually recalled.

Or a few obsessions. A man in the dark listening
to voices: his voices, his that are not his and yet are.

Retelling his life as remembered. Little things.

Mother scowled and father cheered him up.
Such things. Because he fell or broke a pane of glass.

* * *

Visiting the cemetery,
Mother's annual timing was impeccable.
Autumn
& leaf-fall & the stench of decay, & obliterating lichen.

The cemetery bell tolled departure time.
The high gates clanked shut. The library awaited.

But the bus-ride home was the true adventure.
Past the dismal forked park where no children played.

Inner City Canal

This water tumbling over the canal locks
pours no redemption as once in times gone by.

Dead dogs and cats float amid the bankside reeds
with plastic bags, beer cans, bottles, other debris.

The revelries of youth have long since past.
The sportive summer boys have swum their last.

Needles of death now litter the ancient towpaths.
Dark bodies crouch under low cavernous bridges.

Only the majestic swans paddle patiently
awaiting the stale bread of strollers & flight to other parts.

Ghosts of those we loved and those we once befriended
hover over the canal's green sludge, directionless & homeless.

Without Farewell

Late autumn dawn slices through the curtains.
The air chills through the slat in the open window.

Winter is on the way. Thinning flesh & blood
remind the body of its diminution.

Dreams recur of the day's momentary encounters:
a face, a voice, a gesture, a slight event.

Times past re-surface, doubtless holding a key
to a door to be opened, but fearfully & hopelessly.

And he said, without being asked,
'She's gone, and she was tired. She'd had enough.'

Memory wheels to the past like a homing bird.
'We had a good life, but she was tired,' he said.

A last thing, taking her to the local pub in a wheel-chair
for a final sip and a goodnight kiss without farewell.

Nothing to say. Nothing to say.
Speechless before death. Nothing to say.

Of Crows in Time of Civil War

i.m. Charlie Donnelly

Crows sweep across these fields of death.
Fratricidal madness,
brotherhood of hates.

Ancient olive trees,
their trunks contorted by age,
slumber in the windless heat,
leaf by leaf,
fed by the dew of blood.

What brought you here?
Those who know are dead.
Your friends
of the grey Dublin of your youth
could not understand,
fearing their own discomfiture.

You loved, not beyond,
but with reason:
reason with its own peculiar passion.

No carrion comfort here
save for the squawking crows
sweeping across these fields of death.

White Marble

White marble chippings
cold crystals of hale
and a small marble hand
reaching from the grave

We strolled as through a park
familiar with these sights
through lane after lane
remarking any change

Farthest from the boundary wall
the opened soil
awaited the latest occupant

Water trickled in the zinc tub
a clepsydra for the unheeding

Always autumn
Rustle of leafage
No holding of hands
A slow silent walk

I can remember no words

No seasonal cold
rattled our bones

The very air was grey

Silence too
on the bus home

Later
at home
I played jackstone
with those marble pieces

The River

Sluggishly the river flows from west to east.
Despite its bridges it divides the city.

North and south are worlds apart.
Some assert even the climates are different.

Those from the north have a different speech
from those of the genteel south.

The genteel of the north await patiently
and contrive their transference to the south.

Meanwhile they do their best to forget
the northern barbarians growing amid their numbers.

In the north the genteel live comfortably
in well-defined, protected compounds.

No one dares speak of this river of divide.
The Emperor is contemplating diverting the river.

As a Confucian he is seeking harmony.
But he knows that the odds are against him.

He always has in mind the Great Wall.

In the Ruins

Today I renovated an old bellows.
polished the wood and oiled the leather;
today, too, I scraped clean and painted black
an iron cooking pot on three thin legs.

I hung the bellows on the whitewashed wall
under Wyndham Lewis' drawing of James Joyce;
the pot I filled with last year's plastic flowers:
roses, dahlias and chrysanthemums.

Our new bric-à-brac assembled here and there
from the heart of this old house
to decorate, relieve the bareness of the room,
rhyme now with Baudelaire's old nurse.

To the eyes of the unknown dead in their ineffable past
the elemental heat and food stand now
as genteel decorous monuments, bric-à-brac:
an old bellows and an old pot painted black

Hoyos del Espino, Ávila

The Old Windows

The old windows secured against the winter winds
though draughts and rain can't block the season out.
Hibernation is an ideal to dream of, but it's only
for lucky bears that dream of salmon at the weirs

leaping to their spawning place and to their end.
Dream on, thinks the old poet snug in his bed,
of nightingales and that happy village life
frozen forever in stone many centuries past.

Spring is on the way and things again will bud to life.
But the old poet in his bed knows he's not a nightingale
or salmon oblivious of its continuum. He knows
what they don't know, nor the villagers at their dance.

The wind rattles the old windows to his annoyance.
There's no keeping the season out, nor his thoughts.

Portent

In this place many years ago
the tower clock chimed
and birds burst from the trees
with the clack of wingbeats

It was only later
that this became a portent

Memory had wrought
its awful magic with time

I saw no eagles tearing
at each other's neck
hovering ominously
above the scene
before departing
their work done

No eagles here
only familiar crows and magpies
the city's scavengers
eye-pluckers of sheep
and garbage rummagers

The death-pluckers

Rural Retreat

Castilian summer

Morning and the sweep of broom
on the granite flags

The sun peers once more
through the glass eye of the tiled roof

Below in the kitchen
the lonely month-old chick
chirps frantically for her lost partner
devoured by rat or dog two nights ago

The voluptuous glow of the pine beams

The hobbled donkey's honking
with the anger in his stoppered seed

Over the snow-tipped mountains
the summer blue

Scenic baubles of the pale urbanite
a vague prayer to the atrophied senses

* * *

But it is the dust on a grey Dublin street
that has taken my mind
blossoming to weed
in cracks in dirty pavements

The shouts of the drovers
and their barking dogs.
Down to the North Wall
and the waiting ships.
The morose trudge of cows to slaughter

Hoyos del Espino, Ávila

The White Swan

There is a snow-white swan
with a red rose on its head

It's floating in the middle of a lily pond

It moves very slowly
scarcely at all
scarcely disturbing the water

Why do I dream of this swan
with the red rose on its head?

Should I wring its neck,
walk on the floating lilies
and grab its long neck
in a vice grip,
pluck off that red rose

and then
and then return to my dream
of a snow-white swan,
its head prostrate on a lily pod
and no red rose on its head?

Village in the Mountains Long Ago

¿Dónde están?
Al pinar.

Where are they?
Gone to the pinewoods.

Who were they?

Inscrutable peasants,
in a village in the mountains
where the sun scorched
for three months,
and,
for the rest,
mostly,
cold chilled to the very marrow.

Eagles floated above the village,
eyeing carrion.

And there was snow in summer
in the mountains
where the *laguna* was,
beyond the hills.

And the gently pungent
scent of thyme
on the slopes of the hills,
above the village
nestled in the hollow.

All things there turned
like the mule-driven mill-stone,
around and around,
as they had always done.

Ubi sunt?

Such things,
among so many.

Ghostly things
that flicker now
as summer swifts
on the brain's circuitry.

The Centenarian Trees

The centenarian trees, skeletal
after the long winter,
are visible from almost every window.
Towering and gnarled, scarred
from countless pruning,
they image the patients of the cancer hospital.

Stripped bare of their summer leafage,
grim in the sharp winter sunshine
that etches them against the pale blue sky,
they hold their ground,
bulging the concrete surrounds
that can't contain them.

* * *

Winter then.
Now Spring.
Their sap
responds slowly to the mild sunshine.
Their leaves bud in a kind of filigree,
delicately, tentatively,
peeping out from their ancient branches,
in a light greenery that deepens daily.

The People's City

*i.m. Neville Johnson, photographer & painter
and for John Minihan*

He captured all the shuttered nooks and crannies
of the people's city, the back lanes of crumbling cottages,
the decayed tenements with their broken fanlights,
the intimacies and rituals of the poor, the children's
street games with hoop and ball and skipping
barefooted to old rhymes of togetherness.

His camera probed with compassion,
absorbing images without explicit comment:
the artist as witness was his only agenda.
The life he saw was too quick for brush and paint
The click of the shutter with painter's eye sufficed.

That city has gone with its peopled poor
who dwell elsewhere, scattered to outlying ghettos
where needle and pill have replaced the old rituals
of games and gods and saints, the wafers
of broken biscuits and stale bread and dripping.

What would his camera now record?

Who will bare witness now as Neville did?

Village Abattoir

Pigs scented blood, felt the nail-tipped prod,
screamed & panicked.

Sheep needed no prod but went compliantly,
even watched with indifference
the slaughter of others,
their neural gyrations on the block
after the short knife's thrust to the brain;
even the skinning & the blood,
dripping into the bucket.

The calf was another matter.

Roped and led up the laneway
to the village butcher's slaughter shed,
it panicked, hoofing out,
butting with its short horns
the assembled villagers.

It escaped then,
down the laneway
into the village centre,
followed by the amused villagers.

A fiesta of carnage.

The village was an absurd *plaza de toros*.

All good fun for the village.
All joined in the crazy round-up,
the butcher shouting his commands
stentorian like a general.

Back in the abattoir,
roped to the wall,
the calf kicked out wildly,
again & again.

The village fiasco ended
with a sneaky hammer-blow to the head.

The calf sank like an emptied sack.

The spectators applauded
the butcher's village cunning.

The Haven I

Through the rain-beaded window
the trees reach beyond the horizon
Through gaps in branch and leafage
the sea and ships as small as toys
in the distance

Amid the trees
above and below
the constant darting
of birds

magpies
thrushes
blackbirds
thrushes
sparrows
swallows
wood pigeons
and
wheeling
overhead
galleons of gulls

Here inside
the atmosphere
is laden
with an invisible
and scentless sedative

Silence
broken only by whispers

as patients float
in a twilight zone of the mind

A tenuous mist
hangs over the distant sea

Remote
that's the word

The Haven II

Although mid-summer
leaves scurry like mice across the sward

Is it just the wind
or the notorious piper
threatening those who come

Inside
the sleeping dead
dreaming
of a horror or a bliss long past

It's mid-summer
and yet the leaves
scurry like mice across the sward

Outside the wind still gusting

The leaves still scurry across the sward

Leaf-fall
mice scurrying across the sward

The misty horizon in the distance
with the toy ferry and cargo ships

Birds darting here and there below
The wind swaying the birches
and the towering evergreens

The birds darting below
The rain-beaded windows
And the leaves scurrying across the sward

II

People, Present & Gone

Stoker Joe

Battered by time and ailments of the flesh,
sleepless pondering the loved dead
and all the unknown dead e*n masse.*

In the factory boiler room where he worked
Stoker Joe kept his eye on the gauge
to know when he should shovel more.

The air inside was dense with sawdust,
timber waste, the heat infernal. Stoker Joe
wore no mask and cared the less.

He hardly spoke to a single soul.
The roaring blaze and thrum of pump
were his sole concern at the hellgate of his work.

But once he spoke of war and what he'd seen.
If you think this is hell, he said, you are mistaken.
The bayonet charge was worse by far for those forsaken.

Old Will Deceased

The small glasshouse he'd built has fallen down.
Its panes lie shattered on its concrete base,
the last remnant of his years of careful toil.

What he grew there was prized by all who knew:
vegetables and flowers beyond their seasons' scope,
even a winter rose despite the blanket snow.

The shed in which he hoarded all his tools,
that too has fallen to the rain and rust;
the attic of his papers, now mould and dust.

In the end he retreated to a kitchen annex
where the gas flames provided all his heat,
his food leftovers from the neighbours' boards.

Complaint was not his style as he endured.
War he witnessed and knew how things can end;
friends of his earlier days were long since dead.

His pipe and tea-stained poteen were his solace
as he reminisced on how things once had been.
Godly or godless he felt somewhere between.

Let us pray for Old Will now deceased,
remember him with kindness now released.

We Are Alive

We are alive. Whatever. We see things we'll never see again.
The most mundane: condensation on the panes of Autumn,
Street leafage multicoloured, squawking magpies,

blackbirds struggling against suburban cats. My familiar
   blackbirds.
The cheeky robins have not yet reappeared. But they will.
   Berries still red.
To hop into the house fearlessly, possessively.

It is not grass that grows in the garden now.
Weeds proliferate as cotton cobwebs indoors.
Seepage. See page. This page. Spiders spin.

Close your eyes for good and these are gone.
Such little things. The endlessly walked-down street
with all the imperfections of its little houses:

loose slates, blocked drains, unpainted doors,
unspeared metal railings, cracked pavements,
unwanted unleafing trees, blocking light and drainage.

This familiar street grows longer with time's passage.
It seems endless, like a cemetery. Residents come
and go like vagrants. Scarcely time to say hello.

But still, not a bad day for this time of year.
How are you today? No worse than yesterday.
Good. We can only soldier on. You're right there.

Will I reach the haven of Bellevue? You'll be lucky my friend.
Meanwhile ramble on in your customary shuffle.
It's a fine day for Autumn, I say. He agrees and smiles.

Mystery Man

I have seen him in odd corners of the city,
in places remote from his regular bar
into which he comes quietly at peculiar times
to have his brandy and just sit, usually
without engaging in conversation.
He is a familiar sight, short in stature,
grey-bearded with a jet-black toupee
like a dyed mop-head, but no one knows
if it is a toupee or his actual hair.
He doesn't read the papers.
He simply stares into his glass of brandy.
No one knows who he is, what he does,
where he lives. He is not old.
He stays for a short time or for the evening,
alone, impassive. No one knows his name.
This is how things have been for years.

Barflies

Day after day they linger at the bar.
They come from near and far
to escape their loneliness
in gossip and drink and the horses:
widowers, estranged from home,
falstaffians, old and middle-aged
delinquents, ex- plumbers, carpenters,
taxi-drivers, life's flotsam.
Their jollity is ritualistic,
There are no intimacies here
and none expected.
They reminisce about the lost world
of the dead and the changed city.
They complain of the weather,
corrupt politicians, the cost of living.
The barmen know them by their habits;
like poor novelists, stereotypes
are sufficient to keep things going.
Their jokes are predictable
and tolerated, a comfort in a world
that always changes for the worse.
Words are a game with which to play

This is their last sanctuary.
The benediction of drink
their extreme unction.

Men under the Railway Bridge

Was he called Johnny Fortycoats,
indicating the plurality of his dress,
or was it Tim Bassett,
who stood there at the pavement edge
in the dark of the railway bridge
with his box of shoelaces,
never speaking or seeking alms?
Just standing there, bearded and dirty and ragged.
Maybe there were two of them,
as there were two bridges
equally dark with the same poor passers-by
who could ill-afford the copper coins
were sought for shoes
laced with string.

Still, some coins were dropped,
perhaps enough at the end of the day
for a hostel night and a bite to eat.
No one asked or knew where these two,
if there were two, not one, came from,
or where they went at the day's end.
This show lasted for some years through all the seasons.
Then, suddenly, they, one or both, disappeared,
Fortycoats and Bassett.
Whereto no one asked or knew.
Their disappearance was hardly remarked.

Suicide

It happens.
Car parked on the empty beach.
Sometimes a note left.
Sometimes not.
Then a slow deliberate walk
into the cold sea.

No previous signs of what would be.
Family stunned, mystified.

Were there signs missed?

That slow
perplexing
deliberate
walk
into the cold sea.

Plenty of time for a change of mind
unlike a mad leap from a bridge
or another's leap from a ship's stern
into the mangling propellers
and the maws of the sharks.

No Neptune of the deep beckoned
nor have those who loved yet reckoned.

The Perfect Lady

after Edward FitzGerald

Declining very fast,
they say.

They say, too, her mind is
in a state of perfect peace,
even beautiful.

She may rally in the summer
but the odds are against her.

The loss of a perfect lady
when she dies.

An Unknown Life

How many times returning despite the barking dog
to check if the cottage door was locked, the gas
turned off? Stooped and black-shawled, her walk
a slow shuffle. Darkness devoured the evening.

She walked quietly into the night toward death.
Whatever joy she'd had was now long spent.
The silence of defeat had overwhelmed her,
but beyond the sourness of bitterness or hate.

Always the same route down familiar laneways,
smelling of poverty, in the dim flickering streetlamps.
There was no talk, no questions. All had been said.

What did she dream in the long cold nights?
Not of the ravenous wolf under the bed
or the cancer eating the poor morsel of her flesh.

Was it a last winter or autumn evening? Unknown.
The wolf waited patiently under the bed.
The hero axe-man of her life was long since dead.

Schoolboy Mitcher

Down at the stairway docking
where the muddy green river
lapped sloppily
against the slimy steps,
the mitching boy baited inedible crabs
with fish-heads tied to twine.

He knew the times
of the river ferry
by the mid-day tolling
of the Angelus bells,
and he could remember,
without understanding,
its mysterious first words:
*R*EGINA COELI
rejoice alleluia.

Releasing the crabs
from the fish-heads
required all his courage.
Claws could sever a finger.

Time to go home.

In the dirty water of the river
he washed away the smell of the crabs
from his grubby hands,
retrieved his hidden schoolbag.

Lilacs on the classroom's May altar,
candle scent and the Virgin's

plaster statue
were out of mind for the time being.

But not the Reformatory
for his criminal absence.

Tu Fu in Templeogue

i.m. Austin Clarke

Mid-autumn and the apple windfall
was abundant that year.
'Take as much as you can,' he said,
'otherwise the worms and birds
will have their fill as is their right.'

In slippered feet he gathered up the apples
while puffing on his ancient pipe.

At the slope of the garden
the river trickled quietly.

'How things have changed,' casually
he remarked. 'I am the last of the Twilighters,
and I say that without regret.
But that's a long story of much malignity.
My dreams are long trodden on.

I was more Tu Fu than Li Po
although I saw in my time as many ghosts as Li Po:
the moon hanging on a tree
and the flash of the tiny kingfisher
and that lady in waiting,
brightness of brightness.'

I had seen his last two books through the press
for him. He knew mortality was pressing.
Yet there were still some things he wished to say
and see in print before the end.

'This house cannot be handed down,' he had written.
'But my poems can,' he said quietly, 'even to the few.'

My daughter and I parted with our bag of apples.
The old poet bade us farewell at the door.

'Take care now, my friend, you don't offend
the good and powerful when you review their books.
You will forget what you wrote but they will remember.
And with malignity.'

For My Eldest Sister Dead by Fire

Who'll be the first to die? she asked.
I said nothing. Late December
and the leaden sky threatened snow.

We'd chanced to meet on a main street,
she on her way home by bus from work.
We hadn't met for months

It's time for one of us to go, she said.
One could see her mind calculating the odds.
Her question was more than a seasonal malaise.

Her mind was occupied with other things than
calendar computations. Countdown, yes,
but many other factors played a part.

He was a happy child, she said. She was smart.
He was wayward. She was kind but foolish.
I loved you all despite our differences.

As for me, I'm a lost soul, she said,
too late for redemption, too late for change.
I argued with her without conviction.

The bar at the end of the street beckoned.
Come for a drink, she said, it's Christmas.
I'll get home safely, don't you worry.

It was our last meeting. I refused. The guilt
of my cowardice still clings to my craven heart.
The fire of life consumed her in the end.

She was the first to go, she little knew,
at the year's first fall of snow in her hometown.

I Am Happy, Happy

i.m. Gerard Manley Hopkins

These were his last words
as he slipped away,
dying in the dirty Dublin he loathed
despite all his compassion,
his chief woe.

His individuality,
the stamp of his Creator on all things,
every leaf, every blade of grass,
the patterns of eddying water,
the shape of a shell or pebble,
movement of cloud,
defying dictionaries
whether they denote or connote,
shelving his obsession,
even his own soul as his Maker
and he fashioned it.

What a price he paid for this
in the dark night of his exile!

And now here,
still in dirty Dublin,
his scarcely legible name,
chiselled on a grimy slab
in the Jesuit communal plot
in a Glasnevin graveyard,
amid the names of his unknown confreres,
his ultimate destination,
unvisited, the remains of that great self,
master of language,
has found its end.

'I am happy,' he said.
In those last words
he looked beyond the grave
and saw his soul that no soil or slab
could occlude in the eyes of his god.

III

The Poet

The Poet as Wild Man

i.m. Patrick Galvin and Mary Johnston

O but he was wild,
drank the overflowing cup of life,
knew no bounds
but those he'd learnt the hard way,
always at a price he was prepared to pay
without complaint,
bad or good luck at the unknown gods' discretion.

Maimed by the afflictions of age,
he stayed buoyant to the end,
wheel-chair fettered, but his eyes still
glinting with mischief at life's mishaps,
mainly his own,
any blame simply the cards he had been dealt.

Poems he wrote and sang to celebrate rebellion,
of rebels like himself
living on the edge of things,
his own future, like theirs, whatever came next day.

And, despite all,
despite his feckless ways,
he was lucky in the end to find a one true love
who stayed the course with humour,
not dismay.

The Gifted Poet

The gift of poetry was his, received and given.
No one will ever know the why or how of it.
From the start he handled words like a master jeweller,
always mindful of the precious gift he had.

But without arrogance, a dedicated monk
in the scriptorium, a meticulous calligrapher,
a servant to something higher than himself.
The god he served, however, was not so kind.

In a time when poets were either ignored
or lost to the academies, he turned to the people
who were no longer those of old who respected poets.

That was the identity he sought above all else.
A mistake that would cost him dearly in the end:
the gifted poet became the public-house jester.

When those he'd entertained departed
to their suburban havens, he was alone
with only alcohol to relieve his solitude.
The past he sought pained him to the bone.

Death of a Poet

i.m. Miguel Hernández

His life was necessary as his death was needless.
No messianic complex drove him
to the redemption of the fellowship of the poor:
he carried their cross of poverty as his burden,
Christ his exemplar if not his god.

Love was his grand passion, not hatred even
in face of the wickedness he witnessed and suffered.

Was it poetry set him on his journey to death,
a poetry that grew from the clay of his being,
a necessity undeniable whatever the consequences?

Man of the earth, his blood the sap of onion,
his smile the benediction of sunshine,
his laughter birdsong, his embrace
of others the roots of growing things.

Fionn: The Poet As Truant

Fionn.
Fair haired.
That was the boy's name.

Aoibhinn beatha an scoláire
bhíos ag déanamh léinn.

He remembered that.

Happy the life of the scholar
reading his books.

Ah, but no.
The boy could scarcely read,
didn't even know the clock then.

The church bell rang at twelve,
midday, Angelus,
his only chronometer.

And it was May,
Mary's month.

An altar in the classroom,
flowers, candles and a *prie dieu*.

The *regina coeli*,
Queen of Heaven,
in Latin only in May
when the midday bell rang out.

He would bring lilac
snatched from a garden.

Not rosemary,
Mary's mauve bloom.

Beyond the home stretch
there were the ships.

Thánaigh long ó Valparaíso.
A ship came from Valparaíso.
He remembered that, too.

That was his dream.

A ship that would take him
into the magic world
of Sinbad the Sailor.
He would stay at the dockside
observing the loading
&
unloading of cargos:
cattle & horses for Europe's tables,
coal from Newcastle
shovelled by dockers
bared to the waist,
black as the coal
they shovelled
in the deep holds of the ships.

Twelve o'clock
and the bell would ring out.

Time to go home.
Say nothing.
There would be school
another time.

It took his mother
a week to discover his truancy.

Common Birds

Common birds, seagulls,
pigeons,
the highflyers,
punctuate
an invisible script
on the pale blue sky;
while thrush,
sparrow,
starling,
magpie
& blackbird,
the lowflyers,
beak for worm
or berry
down below,
on hedge, in earth.

The poet
sits on his garden bench,
looking up,
looking down,
pondering the invisible
script of the sky,
the sprouting weeds
of his untended garden.
He is remembering
poets he loved
who noted such things.
Swallows,
nightingales
& rooks
homing to oblivion.

Sumer Is Icumen In

for Theo

Time now to hear
the barking of seals
on the strips of beaches,
the gannets screeching
along the cliff-face,
the crash and thud of waves
against the boulders
below.

The sea stretches away
from the island headland
to an horizon blurred
and waving
in the summer mist.

Solitary in his cell
the monk indites
in the margin of his script
his poem of thanksgiving
for Summer's return.

The Poet As Pub Singer

for JB

The Dublin town of streets and pubs were his,
walked in, drunk in, as if born to be its chronicler,
from Coombe to cradle to grave, he hoped,
a good singer and musician to see him out.

The mystery of his life was his alone.
Singing took precedence above all else,
even the countless women he bedded
who fell for his passion and for his charm.

Despite the countless yarns he told, always
with names, places and times recalled
in precise detail and accuracy, he was reticent;
the personal door of his silence had no key

for any who thought they had figured him out.
A wayward boy, his mother and father thought,
who would come to no good in any regular way.
Life was a game he played to his own rules.

His Muse was song who visited him
at inappropriate times, at closing time in bars
where silence after hours was law;
but, eyes shut, he heard her siren voice

and ignored the threats of the barmen guards
and customers who heard no siren sing,
but gluttonously gulped into an alcoholic haze,
uncaring of the Muse whom he amazed.

Trinity of Faces

i.m. Brian Coffey

'The head of this three-faced man
on its statuary plinth
could be that of a poet,' Brian says.
'Left, right and centre,
his vision focused as needs be
but equally peripheral.'

The poet as witness,
storer of memories,
adept in the tricks of memories,
the subjective dictates of feelings,
the ambiguity of language,
still always persistent in self-honesty
and the larger truths
of the void or redemption.

He looks at us now,
stony-faced.
And we try to imagine
what he saw and felt,
what gods or kings were his,
what events he witnessed.

We reinvent him now
in our own image,
using the blankness of ignorance.

The curator modestly speculates:
'It may the face of an unknown god.'

Poet as Outsider

i.m. James Clarence Mangan

The odd figure with witch's conical hat
and birdlike cape unfit for rain or flight,
a wraith of a man strolling the city streets,
our Dublin flâneur
in search of drink or laudanum drops
to anaesthetise his inscrutable misery.

His few friends did what they could to allay
his wretchedness but could not reach
the core of his unhappiness.

The demon of poetry possessed him.

He could not sing ditties like Tom Moore
in fashionable salons where ladies and gents
wept sentimentally into their cups
of claret. Nor would he have been welcomed.

Maturin with a lighted candle on his head
when composing was his compatriot.

Wilde, too, for all his social aplomb,
had that same Irish, rebellious streak.

Joyce went mad with words.

Their musicality was their defence
against the intolerable pain of unbelonging.

Death of an Old Poet

i.m. Antonio Machado

Was it that long trek to Colliure did him in?
More likely tiredness of age and a broken heart.
The gentlest of men, the gentlest of poets,
wise as an old Taoist, knowing right from wrong.

No fame brought him swagger, for he knew better.
The modesty of the common man was his style,
observing the toiling labourers in the fields
as he trudged the ancient landscapes of Castile.

The flamencos his father collected were the sadness
he rewrote to his own mournful tunes for the early
death of his first love for whom he endlessly grieved.

While he was dying in that cheap hotel in Colliure
his old mother was dying upstairs, neither knowing
of the other's impending death, both slipping away
quietly as their wont. Had he known or what he thought,
what he might have said, cannot be known.

Only the words he wrote remain, his lamentations
of the bitterness of men, for which he had no answer.
He knew right from wrong to the end and that's enough.
And he had hope, for which, modestly, he paid the final price.

IV

Reflections of a Sun to Come

The Envoy's Soliloquy

after the Chinese

Names now fall from memory
autumn leaves

I remember places and faces
with the pain of absence

What is a history without names
I ask myself without answer

For dates I consult not the calendar
but the mirror

What I see there looks back at me
the stranger I have become

The winter chill
Blood cooling in the arteries

It's been a long journey
and I have been a poor envoy

The Emperor's advisers will not be pleased
They demand written names and dates
Reports on taxes and malpractice
not weather reports
and reminders of mortality

That least of all

Dismissal faces me on arrival
I can count on that

Nothing of consequence to report
Things are as they always were

The authorities will not be pleased with that

My wife and children
will scarcely know me
it's been so long

Still I hear the gibbons cry
and the lap of water on the riverbanks
and moonlight on its still surface

Such things are little to report

Of Youth and Age

after Robert Frost

That tree must come down.
It blocks the light both summer and winter.

It was planted as a mini-evergreen
but now towers as high as the very roof.

Something so little to begin with
now casts a dark shade on this small house.

My procrastination kept it there
for years; untended nature did the rest..

Despite a showery summer
I took out saw
an axe for the surgery.

The living sap was resistant.
Saw chewed like toothless gums.

Blunted axe merely chipped the bark
and sawdust fell like white tears.

But my energy fell as the tree stood firm.
I've been here for thirty years, it seemed to say,

and I've more time than you to last the day.
I block your light but shelter from wind and rain.

It was an argument I could not easily disdain.
My resolution weakened, prepared to yield.

Then three kids stopped at the garden gate:
sixteen, eleven and four I guessed their age.

'I'll saw for you,' the handsome eldest boy offered.
'You look more tired than that tree you want cut down.'

'No,' I said. 'I'll cut the damn thing down.
It makes my life more gloomy than myself.'

So once again I took to saw and axe,
growing weaker as my determination passed.

'OK, lads,' I said at last. 'It's your turn now.'
This to the eldest boy with care.
In seconds he was through the garden gate,
saw in hand and jagging through the bark.

'We're nearly there, it's nearly down,' he said
as he hacked away this way and that.

We roped the tree to take it from the house
so when it fell, it would fall away from harm.
It fell then when I was chasing off a cat
'No harm done,' the boy remarked.

'It's gone for good now and won't now block the light.
It just needed that little bit of strength.'

Write Something Happy

Write something happy, I was urged.
And I've tried as best I could.

Life for life's sake.
The smallest of pleasures would suffice.

The past is something to forget:
the future has not occurred, yet.

How goes the night, the porter asks.
Well, I reply, despite the raven's croaking
above the battlements.

He pisses against wind with great relief,
little knowing there's murder in the wind.

How sweet the air is here.
Sleep well, my lord. All is well.
Tomorrow the sun will shine on a new day.

The night-owl hovers above its prey.
But that's its nature.
Life for life's sake.

His happiness is that momentary relief.
Goodnight, my lord, and sleep well.

But there's murder in the wind
against which he pisses.

Let's Soldier On

The old platitude we use again and again
though it means less and less as time goes by.
We must pay the price for having loved so deeply.
Would it have been better not having loved at all?

To have kept our distance from others and ourselves,
not living but going through the motions of a life.
Hello, Goodbye, ships passing in the night
and the cold sea between us. Little lights in the distance.

Destinations unknown.
                        Flares in the darkness;
not for mariners now but soldiers on the fields of death
waiting for their officer's command, revolver in hand,
facing the recalcitrant and fearful.

'We soldier on,' he barks. 'You can't go back or stay.
Fix bayonets, get ready for the fray.'

La Vida Es Sueño

Are we mere stuff as dreams are made of.
We dream even ourselves
until the dream ends
and we pass then into the dream of others,
of those we loved or loved or hated us.
The dictate of history?
Another dream,
the nirvana of nothingness not even nothing?

A dream trapped in a dream,
a tiger dream of tooth and claw.
Surrounding sight and smell of blood.

The Greater Grace

for Irene

Remembrance. Charity or even love
remembered, reminded,
is lost to gratitude. The deed done
must be forgotten. The token proffered,
given and forgotten. Once spoken,
is lost or turned to resentment,
an exposed weakness, unwelcome.

Forgive me, O lord, not for my sins
but for lack of love, your grace.
Reward is in the loving,
not from the receiver.
My lack is your greater need;
what I give is my need not yours.
To forget is the greater grace.

Last Words of the Old Atheist

What were the last words of the old atheist on his deathbed
as the nurse put him on the morphine drip to see him
through to the oblivion he had told everyone
he could face without fear and always knew would be the end?

No Nirvana or Absolute for him. Simply a shutting down
of the brain. Perfectly natural and inevitable
he had always reasoned with that third brain
of the neo-cortex. Those he loved & loved him

waited patiently at the bedside. A few of them waited,
like dear Emily, for a sign of the departure
of the soul or ghost, such things he himself
had rejected as delusions of the neural circuitry.

But the fuse blew before he could bid a last farewell:
a last sick joke but thoroughly reasonable no doubt.

Major or Minor

To celebrate the quotidian is admirable:
all the little things that keep one going.

Even more daring is to deal with the big things:
finding God or coping with the Void,
facing the Joycean nightmare of history.

The days of major or minor are long gone
despite the academies and their categories.

Shakespeare was not God, nor was Dante,
nor Homer: the great trilogy of Western majors.

Better Li Po or Tu Fu looking with admiration
at the moon or remarking the gibbon's cry;
or Chuang Tzu wondering whether he was a butterfly.

Or the lament of the conscript at the Great Wall,
missing his home, wife and children.

Major or minor? Aquinas pondering
the dance of angels on the needle's point,
Pascal pondering endless space?
Descartes' pineal gland, Kant's *Critique*?

A lonely man looks into the muddy water
of a city canal and wonders what lies beyond it.

He knows he is nobody but still wonders.
There it is. No question of major or minor.

Street Rhymes

for Andrea

1

Jinny Joe, Jinny Joe,
hiding in the grass,
waiting for the wind to blow
ignoring all who pass.

Where do your babies go
when the winds blow?
Wherever they can find
a place in which to grow.

In nook or in cranny
in concrete or in tile:
they need very little
to keep themselves alive.

2

If I had a little donkey
and he wouldn't go,
would I beat him?
No, no, no!

I'd put him in a stable
to keep him nice and warm,
for he's best little donkey
that ever was born.

3

I had a little singer
who couldn't grow any bigger,
so I put him in the window
for a show.

But he lifted up the window
and broke his little finger
and he couldn't play his old banjo.

4

The moon shone bright
and silvered the water
and I thought it was made of glass.

I looked at myself
with great delight
and found I was a foolish ass.

5

A robin came into my garden
to see what he could find.
He looked here and there
but found nothing to eat
so he came into my house to dine.

A Single Word

A play with words is a play with worlds.
A single word evokes a dream world,
of places where I have never been,
peopled with faces I have never seen.

Or with faces long faded but not forgotten.
Mouths open in a gabble of speech
that says nothing I can understand:
intimate ghosts beyond our reach.

It is their faces that beckon their invitations.
I miss you dearly, my love. It is
unfair we should have parted despite our love.

This love that binds and separates with pain.
I am alone here without your love,
waiting hopelessly for us to meet again.

Grey Rain

i.m. César Vallejo

Dense haze of grey rain
filling the narrow street
of terraced houses

Then
an apparition
an instant framed picture

The window assumed
the old man
in the middle of the street

yoked to his barrow of turf
wet and dumb
stopped by a pebble
and the ache of years

Something from my own past
from childhood and poverty
from present nightmare

I stop writing

The Spanish words of Neruda
retreat to the dictionary

Hoyos del Espino, Ávila

Lady Morphia

'Doctors, doctors,' he exclaimed,
'admit Lady Morphia
to attend at my bedside
and anoint me with her tears
of compassionate relief.

My mouth is open with pleading,
my veins are bulging with desire.
I have so long awaited her coming
you should not deny her admission.

She will enfold me in a dream
beyond your comprehension,
beyond your care, however
attentive.

Angel of death,
she comes smooth as silk ,
soft and dark as pillowed-down,
summer twilight.

All my fears,
all my pain,
will be dispelled
at the first influx of her tears.'

Castilian Rhymes

Pedro and Fidel
in heaven or hell
with their goats
and their sheep
lost now in my sleep.

Whatever befell
Pedro and Fidel?
In Gredos they dwell
whether heaven or hell.

The tinkle of bell
sounds for Pedro and Fidel
lost in the mountains
they knew so well.

Ice and fire
can't cast their spell
on these rugged men
whether in heaven or hell.

Winter Muse

Mid-winter frost whitens the roofs,
the garden walls and hedgerows.
Even the uncut grass of late summer
shows a hoary head of weeds.

I peep out the window
at the uninviting scene outside,
but quickly return to the warm bed
where my muse lies fast asleep and snoring.

Love beckons in this cold climate.

But it will soon be dawn
with a little sunlight
to melt the frost
if not unfreeze the chill.

A last peep outside
to watch the early blackbirds
poking for worms in the frozen earth.

Love Is the Unspoken

Love is the unspoken

Once said
it becomes something else

Love is endurance
all embracing

Do I contradict myself?
That too is love

Does love have an ending?

In bitter fights
and the most vicious of words?

That too is love.

Is love an animal interdependence?

That too is love

Shall we meet again in the hereafter
as in the early years of love?
Young and lustful as once we were.

Very debatable or even desirable.

Can we change love as we change a car?
It happens.

Is love a bad habit?
Based on concealed secrets?

Te quiero the Spaniards trot out

Love is enduring remembrance
from that first glance
to the end

It is a word signifying all

www.ingramcontent.com/pod-product-compliance
Lightning Source LLC
Chambersburg PA
CBHW030048100426
42734CB00036B/578